Sara Eliza Wiltse

Myths and Motherplays

Sara Eliza Wiltse

Myths and Motherplays

ISBN/EAN: 9783337177126

Printed in Europe, USA, Canada, Australia, Japan

Cover: Foto ©ninafisch / pixelio.de

More available books at **www.hansebooks.com**

MYTHS and MOTHERPLAYS

BY

SARA E. WILTSE

AUTHOR OF "STORIES FOR KINDERGARTENS," "A BRAVE BABY, AND OTHER STORIES,"
"PLACE OF THE STORY IN EARLY EDUCATION," ETC.

———

ILLUSTRATED WITH TWENTY-FOUR FULL-PAGE DRAWINGS

BY

HIRAM PUTNAM BARNES

———

MILTON BRADLEY COMPANY
SPRINGFIELD, MASS.
1895.

CONTENTS.

LIST OF ILLUSTRATIONS.

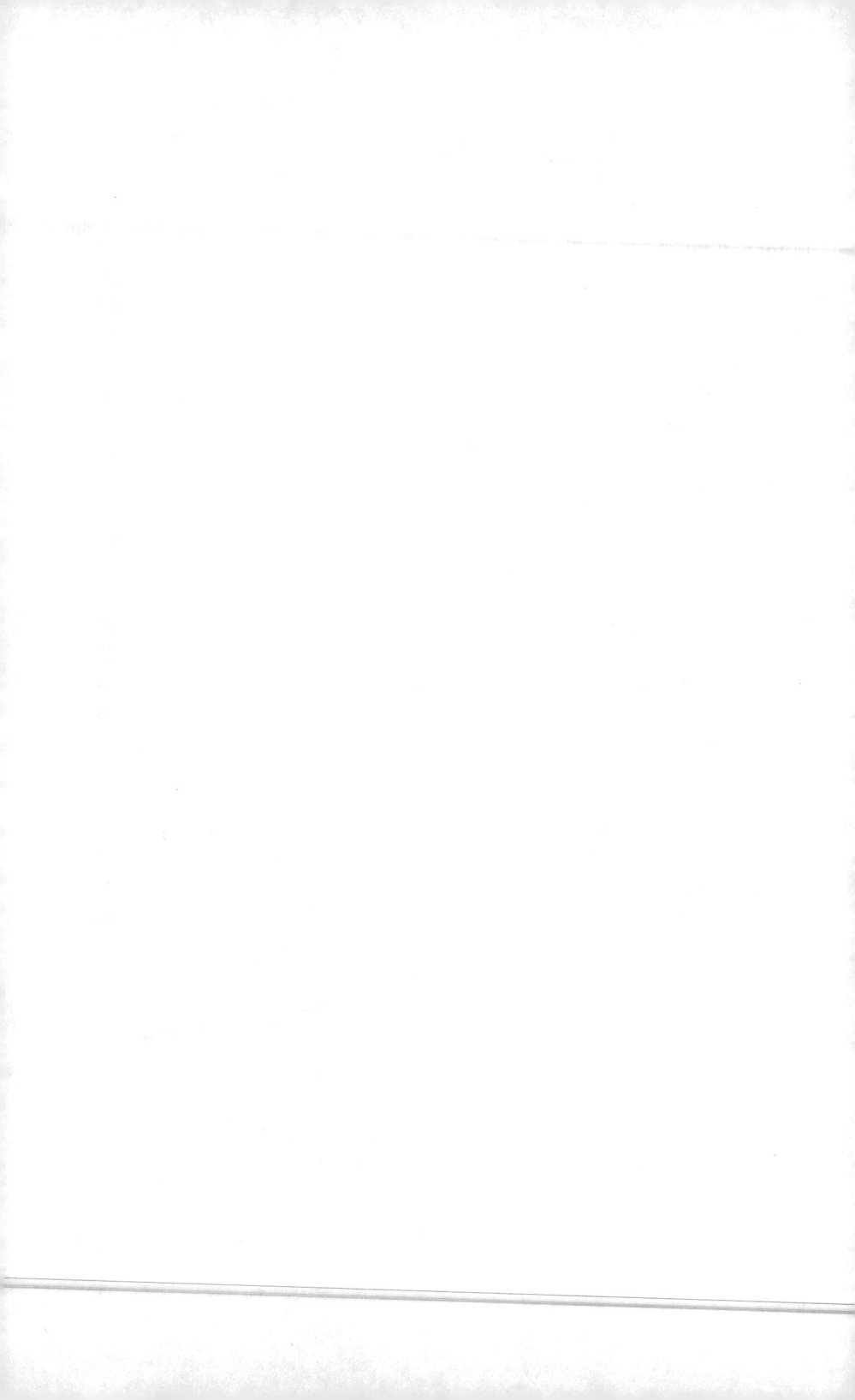

PREFACE.

The relation between classic nature myths and Fröbel's Motherplays has heretofore been almost unnoticed. If any kindergartner exclaims, "I always told rainbow stories when we made bridges!" or, "Of course I told one or more sun myths when we played with our prisms!" then I shall have added assurance of the pedagogical value of the work undertaken in this book.

I have given twelve groups of nature myths suited to the twelve months of the year, hoping the kindergartner may suggest to the mother the desirability of drawing the child's attention to the phenomena of nature which is particularly noticeable in July and August when the child is not in kindergarten.

To select myths for very young children, eliminating every harmful element, while preserving the spirit, and as far as possible, the letter of such ancient literature, has been a grave task. In many instances I have been able to give little but the great central thought about which the ages have wrapped masks and cerements quite unfit for the child to handle, for valuable as our folk lore is to the mature mind, much of it I consider most pernicious for the children.

It will be observed that I have carefully told these stories, as *stories*, and not as facts. To me it seems more rational to be truthful, and after many years of close study of children, and considerable practise in story telling, I am convinced that imagination is not cramped nor pure joy in the wildest fiction decreased by the cautious beginning of tales with the saving clause — "people used to think, or some people believe."

To keep to the golden mean is very difficult, to be misunderstood and misinterpreted is very easy, but it would seem as if these stories as here arranged might be given by any teacher who has the spirit of the little child within herself, with untold benefit not only to the child of vivid imagination but to the stolid one whose imagination needs quickening.

THE AUTHOR.

MYTHS AND MOTHERPLAYS

SUN MYTHS

ONCE upon a time when all the world was young, men, women and children used to tell each other many stories. They told of a land far to the South, which was so bright and hot that no one could enter it who was not born within its fiery borders. From a spark of this fire-world they thought the sun was made, and placed in the sky world to light the earth. As the sun seemed to move across the sky these children of the young world thought it must be drawn by horses, and they could sometimes see the forms of these swift steeds in the clouds.

A story once begun grows like Jack's bean-stalk, and when one had seen the

horses, another could see the chariot, and having given the Sun a chariot and horses, some poet child caught a glimpse of a bright maiden guiding these, and she was called the wife of "The Shining One."

In another country the children of long ago thought the early morning light was a sweet maiden whom the Sun loved and lost. His journey across the heavens was a daily search for her, and out of this story grew one of the most beautiful thoughts ever cherished in men's hearts: the thought that the Sun, although sorry for his loss, and never ending his search, kept doing his work for the earth from day to day so that no little earth flower, however humble, missed one ray from the generous, life-giving center of light and heat.

THE LIGHT BIRD.

ET us look at the picture before mamma teaches us the song. A little child is holding a mirror in the sunshine, and the light is thrown on the wall under the window; when the mirror is moved the light seems to flit about like a bird, and the baby tries to catch it. You can do this with a basin of water, or with a prism, which will give you a light bird with all the colors of the rainbow. But you can never catch and hold this bird in your hand, or hide it in your pocket.

One child is holding a ball for the kitten to play with: The kitten is pleased when the ball is lifted above her reach and will leap for it and run after it as long as the child can play. These children are very happy, and it is a good and sure way they are taking to be happy; one in amusing the baby and the other full of joy in amusing the kitten.

If there is the sunshine of love in our hearts we will never spend a day without giving pleasure or comfort to somebody or some thing, and children are quite able to add more to the happiness of this happy world than is possible for any grown person, no matter how rich or powerful the grown person may be.

The little boy on the ladder is trying to catch a real bird, but it has flown. He could not get the bird's song to hold in his hand, even if he caught the bird. Look at the mother in the picture. She is surely a very loving mother, and her children see that; but the love is like the light bird, and can give them happiness even when the day is cloudy, and the loving mother away from home. For love stays in our hearts, and grows brighter and brighter the more we do for each other.

THE LIGHT BIRD.

MOON MYTHS

GREEK children used to tell this pretty story about the moon :

A moon maiden loved a shepherd lad, and often went to see him when he was tending his flocks. But he was taken away from the sky world one day, and she could not find him.

Being a brave, true-hearted maiden she lost no time in crying, but said : "Here are his sheep and lambs left without care. I will watch them, feed them, and give them water from the fountain until he comes." So to this day she is sometimes called the shepherdess.

Hindoo children used to hear a moon story, quite as pretty.

One of their gods was said to have come to earth in the form of a poor man. While walking one day he lost the path and became very tired and hungry.

At last he met a little rabbit, and asked food of him. The rabbit said, " I eat only grass, which is not fit for you."

" I am very hungry," said the man ; " but I cannot eat grass."

The rabbit was sorry for the hungry man, and said, "I am only a little rabbit; but you may eat me."

Then the man took the rabbit in his arms, and caressed him, saying: "Little friend, you offered yourself to a god; great shall be your reward."

And holding the happy little animal on one arm, he drew a picture of a rabbit upon the moon, and restoring the creature to earth, said:

"There is your picture in sight of all men for all time, and you shall be remembered forever as an unselfish rabbit."

Some children think they see the picture of a rabbit in the moon whenever they look for it.

In Africa when the new moon is expected, whole tribes of people hurry out to look for the first gleam of the silver crescent, and when it shines forth, every man, woman and child shouts the word Kua!

But the most fascinating moon story is found in Egypt. It was believed there that the moon-god, Thoth, once wrote a book. The book was filled with stories of everything on earth, in the sea and even in the air. Not a beast, bird, or fish but had a true story about it, which if read by any man, would enable him to charm the world. Thoth, however, did not publish his stories, nor even tell them to his wife, or promise to tell them to his children; but he put them in a box of gold, locked the gold box in a casket of silver, shut the silver casket in ebony and ivory, sealed the ebony and ivory within a case of bronze, hid the case of bronze in a chest of brass, concealed the chest of brass in a little iron safe, which was no doubt a self locker, and threw the whole into the river Nile, from which no man has ever taken it, because no man can find it. But do not cry over the lost stories, my dear children, for if the legend of them were true, and you could get the very book from the golden box, I doubt if you would find the stories of the Moon-god Thoth quite as good as those you tell each other; because nothing that has power to charm the world and do good can be crushed into an iron safe and entirely covered for centuries under the waters of any river.

So Thoth only hid a little parchment and metal after all, for the story of stories is still open to the eyes and hearts of children who keep the key of all mysteries — ask mamma if it is not so.

THE LITTLE BOY AND THE MOON.

THIS little boy has been looking at the moon, and what do you think he is begging his mamma to do?

He thinks if he climbs the ladder he will be able to reach the beautiful shining ball and hold it in his hand.

You can see the castle which is higher than the ladder, and the moon higher than all.

Babies often reach for the moon with their little hands. I knew a baby who soon learned he could not grasp it even when his papa held him high as he could reach; but this baby had played with the light bird, and was happy in seeing many things which he could not touch, and so he laughed and kissed his little hands to the moon, just as he did to his mamma when she was leaving him.

There are so many poems about the moon that each child might have one to recite; but there is a single line written long ago by a man who must have had a child's heart. We learn that : —

"The moon looks on many night flowers, the night flowers see but one moon."

Or this, which is older yet : —

"Late, late yestere'en I saw the new moone
Wi' the aulde moon in her arms."

The children's own poet, Wordsworth, tells how he looked at the new moon when he was a child, and thought it was a silver boat in the sky's boundless sea of blue; sometimes he thought it was a crown of pearls, and then again he imagined it was a lovely woman wrapped in a veil of fleecy clouds.

Surely some children can understand that our thoughts go up and down an unseen ladder of love, so that nothing beautiful in all this beautiful world is quite out of reach, if we will be unselfish in our thoughts as well as in our acts.

THE LITTLE BOY AND THE MOON.

WIND MYTHS

IF you will put your ear against a telegraph or telephone pole when the wind is blowing you will hear what the children of the Old World thought was the music of the wind gods. You can hear it among the pine-trees and the dry leaves of the oaks in winter. A bit of wire stretched firmly across one of your windows will make a harp for Æolus.

When the Old World children heard the whispering winds in the reeds or among the trees they thought a god was there, and they told each other these stories about him:

A child was born in a cave, and in three hours he had grown to be a man. Going out into the world he made a lyre from a tortoise shell from

which he drew such music that the flowers swayed back and forth in a mystic dance in which all the birds and beasts joined. Then the very stones heard and leaped from the earth in a merry round, and as the musician's heart grew more and more joyous in giving joy to others his powers increased until he called the very dead from their resting places.

Then wonder of wonders ! his music reached the hearts of people who were doing wrong, and they dropped their evil ways and joined the happy throng of singers.

I will not try to tell you all the names this god was given, for in each country he was called by a different one, and his history differs in various languages.; but if you remember that sound is the one name upon his forehead, then you will be able to know him whether he carries a reed pipe or a tortoise lyre.

But the winds are not always gentle, and the hurricane must also take on a visible form ; so we have stories of the grinders and crushers who are clothed in rain. In their hands are fiery daggers, and you may hear their whips as they go upon their way ; they roar like lions and the mountains shake beneath their tread.

Of them an ancient poet wrote : " On what errand are you going, O winds ? Lances gleam upon your shoulders, anklets on your feet, and golden cuirasses on your breasts ; lightnings blazing with fire glow in your hands, and golden tiaras are towering on your heads."

Even the modern poets speak of the winds as if they were like ourselves, having hands and feet. Mrs. Deland, who writes so beautifully of the flowers and seasons, says —

> The morning winds on unseen feet
> Over the hilltops lightly pass.

THE WEATHER-VANE.

If you have some feathery seeds from the milk-weed, or a downy feather, or even some shreds of tissue paper, place one of them in the palm of your hand, and you can blow it away with your lightest breath. Or you can blow upon a pin-wheel as the wind blows upon the windmill.

See the weather-vane on the church steeple in the picture ; perhaps you can see a real weather-vane when you go to walk, but you might blow with all your might and you could not turn it as you move the feather in your hand.

Look at the flag in the picture, the kite and the tree bending over ; then look out-of-doors at the real things moved by the wind. You can play your hand is a weather-vane, and you can turn it back and forth. What wonderful thing is this you are doing ?

Turning your little hand like a weather-vane without blowing upon it ? And now you turn your hands round and round very swiftly like a water-wheel, but neither wind nor water is moving them !

What does move them ? And you can turn your head, and swing your arms ! Some wonderful power must be about ! With this power in you, you might hold your hand out in a very strong wind, and say :

" You are very strong, Mr. Wind, but you cannot turn my hand on the joints of my wrist as I can do it. See ! it moves only when *I* will. You are very great and powerful, and you can do many things with trees which I am not strong enough to do, but at the same time, little as I am, I can make more wonderful movements than you, for I do greater things than to move my hands to and fro : I *think* before I *do*, and nearly everything I do is done because I love my mamma, and sometime I will understand just what she means when she sings : —

" Whichever way the wind doth blow,
Some heart is glad to have it so;
Then blow it east, or blow it west,
The wind that blows, that wind is best."

"OTHER THINGS THAT THE WIND DOES."

RAIN MYTHS

THE children of the Old World told each other quaint stories about the rain.

Sometimes there were long, dry seasons when the earth became parched, fruits withered and flowers drooped in the long grass.

But these poet-children forgot their own needs in thinking about the rain sister, who was stolen from earth and locked in a black cloud or cave in the upper air. They knew a god or a giant would set her free, and when a flash of lightning blinded their eyes, they laughed and were glad, for they thought it the lance of Indra, who was coming to free the rain sister.

Other children thought that Zeus sometimes went about the sky like a white swan, and when many little snowy clouds floated about, they called them the swan sisters, but Zeus, the brother, could change himself from a swan to a golden shower.

There is a pretty story of the rainy sisters having been changed into doves, and placed in the sky.

We shall hear more of these sisters when we study the star myths, for we shall see that the sun, moon, stars, rain, clouds and all we love to-day in nature was thought to belong to one family, and we may well wish that we, like the Aryans, Hindus and Greeks, might be so childlike in heart as to call the stars and clouds our brothers and sisters.

April — the opener of earth and cloud — is our little rain sister, and we all know the old rhyme about her :

> " April showers
> Bring May flowers."

Some of the very oldest stories about the rain clouds are the loveliest. The children of the old, old world, looking at the dark clouds scudding overhead, and hearing the low rumble of thunder, thought some giant was driving the cattle into a cave.

We have seen how quickly a story grows from a single pretty thought, and we can understand how natural it would be to make long stories about these cows — you can make a whole book of them yourselves, and you will no doubt explain the rain-fall just as they did, by saying the cloud cows are being milked, and many a thirsty flower on earth gets a refreshing drink of milk when the giant's pail overflows.

There was another thought about the rain clouds which is very beautiful. Some poet-child, catching a glimpse of the bright sun, as the clouds parted for a moment, called it a golden egg, and thought the dark storm-cloud was a wonderful bird, hovering over her beautiful egg of pure gold.

You have in these old thoughts enough material for stories of your own to make you and all your playmates happy during many a rainy day, and your own pretty variations of the story of the rainy sisters, of Zeus, and his reason for changing from a swan to a golden shower, of the cattle that bellow in the cloud caves, of the golden egg hidden under dusky wings, and some new thought entirely your own may serve as good purpose as these old stories have served.

BO-PEEP.

THERE are so many charming ways of playing bo-peep and hide-and-seek, that one hardly need tell the children about them.

Perhaps the little child hiding behind the shrubbery does not know that grown people dearly love to play this game.

The baby that hides its face behind a handkerchief, or pulls its mother's cloak about it, and laughs with delight in the game, before it has learned to say "peep," will enjoy hiding behind a door when it is old enough to walk.

The child that creeps under the sofa, or crouches behind a chair, and calls, "Now find me, mamma," will carry the same spirit of fun and love of hiding into youth and even manhood.

Sometimes when tall boys come home from school they will go into a room softly, and sit behind a screen, or in a corner, and remain unseen until mother or sister says : " It is quite time that boy should be home, is it not ? " and then he laughs gleefully, and says, " I am here."

Once upon a time a woman — quite an old woman too, — had an unexpected visitor, and when she saw her husband coming to dinner she said to her guest : " Now, hide in the closet, and I will send him there to get his slippers, and he will be surprised to find you there."

The guest, who was so old that she had gray hairs, squeezed herself into the closet, and when the white-haired man came in, his wife said : " Dinner is about ready ; but you must be tired ; get your slippers from the closet, and make yourself comfortable."

But the man said : " Thank you, I do not care to put on my slippers now." After a moment she said : " Will you please hand me my white shawl from the closet before we go to dinner." That made the man laugh, for she already had the shawl on. And the visitor in the closet laughed, too, and the man, hearing some one laugh in the closet, of course found the hidden visitor.

All this made them very joyous, and at dinner they asked the children if they had found any new ways of playing the dear old games.

AND LAUGHS WITH DELIGHT IN THE GAME.

FLOWER MYTHS

Norse children used to believe that the flowers grew only when Freya walked, and that if the earth were frozen and without a blade of grass it would become warm and flowery if she came down for a journey across the world. Our Maiden-hair fern is still called Freya's hair in Iceland, and no doubt some child there has a pretty belief of its own about these lovely tresses which others call Our Lady's Hair, in memory of Mary, the mother of Jesus.

The Greeks held sacred all flowers that grew in hidden nooks in the depths of the forests, believing · they were there for the goddess Diana. The ancient Norsemen believed the gods brought the flowers, while the Hindus thought the flowers brought the gods.

We have learned how the Norse people believed the touch of Freya's foot upon the earth would cause the flowers to spring into life. The Hindus believed that from the lotus flower came their god Brahma, and in Egypt this flower was held sacred more than four thousand years ago.

The lily-of-the-valley is sometimes called May-lily. In New England we call the trailing arbutus May-flower, but in some parts of England the lilac is called May-flower.

There are many games and rhymes with and about flowers that belong especially to children.

The dandelion which is just beginning to blossom is known to many of them as the "blow ball," because they like to blow the feathery seeds from the stalk to learn the time of day, saying :

> "One o'clock, two o'clock; it's time we were away."

It has also been called the peasant's clock, its flowers opening very early in the morning. The hollow stem is often split and rolled with the tongue, making long, fair curls or ear rings.

The flowers need the sunshine, and some of them turn on their stems so that they face the sun all day. The children of the Old World soon learned this, and it is not strange that they thought the flowers loved the sun as the child loves its mother.

Many flowers close their petals when the sun goes down at night, and this gave rise to a number of pretty stories.

Flowers and fairies must belong to each other, and it is no wonder that people still think of dancing elves when they see the little rings of greener grass in a meadow of emerald hue.

Some country people used to believe that if they stepped upon a certain flower after sunset, a fairy horse would appear and carry them about all night.

Our marsh-marigold, which we call the cowslip, is known to some children as the fairy cup, and German children call it the key flower, and have a pretty fairy story about it.

We have our own quaint fancies about certain leaves and flowers which will sometime become ancient flower lore.

THE GARDENER.

Perhaps the first thing you will notice in this picture is the little girl watering flowers, but the clock in the tower has told her it is the right time to do this, for

> "Watering in the sun's hot glow
> Never makes the flowers grow;"

and we must all learn that there is a right time for every kind act. Even the sun goes behind the clouds when the rain is falling on the flowers and waits his turn in taking care of them. But when we first sow our flower seeds it is very hard to leave them alone, we are so anxious to help them grow; but while we let the earth and the sun and rain do their share we can play garden by making a lily bud with the fingers of ours left hand, and a watering pot with our right hand, making believe the thumb is a spout from which the water falls upon the lily. The little boy in the picture has gathered some of his flowers to give to the old man who is passing.

Perhaps the man thinks of an old verse :

> "There is a garden in the fall
> Where roses and white lilies grow."

Suppose a child lives in a city where he cannot have a garden or even a pot of flowers, what can he give to make people's hearts glad? Something which may blossom in the coldest air; frost cannot put it to sleep, nor rain drown it. Something grown people would not like to be without even if offered acres of roses in its place. None but children can give the very sweetest of these gifts, so they should be generous with them. What is it?

A child's joyous smile and pleasant voice.

Care for your own heart garden " where these grow " and we shall have the best of flowers all the year.

Here is a pretty verse known to most kindergarten children :

> "Kind hearts are the gardens,
> Kind thoughts are the seeds,
> Kind words are the blossoms,
> And the fruits are kind deeds."

"WATERING IN THE SUN'S HOT GLOW
NEVER MAKES THE FLOWERS GROW."

·TREE·AND· STREAM· ·MYTHS·

LONG ago when men and women had only the knowledge of little children, they were fond of asking questions. There were always a few poets and story-tellers in every country who were ready with answers to all that could be asked. We know they sometimes made mistakes, but their mistakes were so beautiful it is no wonder they were believed to be true. The Norsemen thought the earth itself was a great ash-tree of which our oaks and elms were but little twigs. Other people of olden times watched the trees bending in the wind and thought gods were hidden within their trunks. The Greeks have a pretty story of Apollo and Daphne which explains the sacredness of the laurel-tree and the wreath of laurel which Apollo wears.

Daphne was a beautiful nymph, daughter of a river god. Apollo saw her, and wished to take her to his home. But Daphne wanted to stay near the stream where her father lived, and in the woods where Diana hunted, so she ran from Apollo, who pursued her. She would not stop to hear him say he was a god, but ran until her strength was exhausted, when she called upon her father to save her ; and just as Apollo was about to overtake her, she was changed into a laurel-tree, and the god of music kissed the tree and said : "Thou shalt be my tree. I will wear thee for my crown, and with thee will adorn my harp. Thou shalt be woven into wreaths for the brows of conquerors, and thy leaf shall know no decay."

People used to think that the great Jupiter spoke to them in the rustling of the oak leaves. Our own beautiful birch-trees were called the white ladies of the forest by the poet Longfellow. Many children of to-day listen for the song of the leaves, and ask again and again what do they say ? And when the branches sway in the breeze they ask what are they doing ? A little boy not yet old enough to read these stories took his first steps in the spring, and would not pass a tree in his walks without putting his arms around it ; this winter every tree he passed received a snow kiss. If a grown poet had walked with this little child and been permitted to read his thoughts, we might have a song sweeter than any yet sung, for trees and flowers and children are just as wonderful as of old. There are trees that are still thought to be made of lightning, and some Scotch milkmaids wear little charms made of the wood of the mountain ash, thinking it protects them from lightning.

There is an old Hindu tree myth which explains this practice. A falcon offered to restore the stolen Soma to the gods. In doing it he lost a claw and a feather. Both fell to earth, and taking root grew into trees, one of the trees having red sap and scarlet blossoms. Because the falcon was himself a lightning god, his feather and claw grew to be sacred lightning trees. The red berries of the mountain ash, being somewhat like the red flowers of the "palasa-tree," it was easy for childlike people to believe it also sacred. The robin also became sacred ; red lightning, red berries and red birds being in some way related to Thor, the god of thunder.

THE NEST.

WHAT do you see in the branches of the tree nearest the house?

Shall I tell you about a nest like that which I once saw in an apple-tree? A pair of robins built the nest, and one of them used to sit in the very highest branch of the tree at sunrise and sunset and sing so sweetly that every one about was glad there was a nest in the tree, for we thought he was singing to please the little mother bird who when her eggs were laid would hardly leave them long enough to rest her wings. After much singing and many days of sitting on the nest there were more listeners to the papa bird's song than you can guess.

There were four little baby birds, that must have listened well, for they grew up to be good singers, too. But there were other listeners to the happy song. A hen who could not sing, but who loved her chickens dearly brought ten of them to live under the apple-tree, and there was another not in this picture, but in the house, who listened every day for the song of the bird, the twitter of the baby birds, the cluck of the mother hen, and peep-peep of the chickens. Who could it be? It was a little child whose mamma told him all about the care every mamma in the world takes of her babies.

She showed the child how to make a little bird's nest with his fingers, putting the thumbs down in the nest for eggs, and letting them fly out as birds. She sang him many songs about birds, and he himself found the blue-bird's nest in the hole in the tree, and showed his mamma a little nest like it, made with his left hand, while his right played it was a number of birds, the thumb was a robin, the first finger a blue-bird, the middle an oriole, the ring finger a swallow and the little finger a sparrow. In the picture you can find a nest for each. You will be pleased with the robin's nest story, for the same papa and mamma robin came year after year to the same nest and found the same child in the house to give them crumbs and listen to their song. One bird built its nest on the ground, but it had no cause to fear the kind children who found it.

"IN THE GRASS, JUST WHERE IT'S BEST,
LITTLE BIRD HAS BUILT ITS NEST."

· RAINBOW MYTHS ·

IF you will look at a rainbow from
the time it appears until it fades from
sight, thinking of the sky, the clouds and
the glorious arch, perhaps you will feel a
little as the Norsemen did when they first
called it Bifrost or trembling bridge, and
believed that the gods came over it from
Heaven to earth. They thought the
bridge was guarded by Heimdall who had
a palace at the highest part. Our own
poet, Longfellow, could think their
thoughts, for he wrote :

" Bifrost i' th' east shone forth in brightest green;
On its top in snow white sheen
Heimdall at his post was seen."

Sometimes they thought the rainbow
was itself the beautiful god, who needed
less sleep than a bird; who could see as

well by night as by day; and could hear the corn growing on the earth, and the soft wool lengenthing on the sheep's back.

The Persians thought the rainbow bridge was guarded by a maiden that when asked who she was, always answered :

" I am thy good thoughts, good words, good deeds."

The Hebrews believed it a sign that God thought of them and all that had happened to them in their troubled lives, especially of a promise made by Him to them. So we see how the thoughts of men grew sweeter as they looked at this glorious arch. First it was a bridge for the gods, then the gods themselves, and to many it now seems a present thought of God.

We will learn to think these thoughts about it, and perhaps we shall then understand about the pot of gold of which all children hear nowadays.

This dear story will not be spoiled for us if we learn to look within our own hearts for our end of the rainbow — our own hearts which are the real golden pots, holding good thoughts which are like trembling bridges ; from which come good words like winged gods, and out of which issue good deeds that are binding promises of still better things.

The children's own poet loved the rainbow, and wrote :

> " My heart leaps up when I behold
> A rainbow in the sky :
> So was it when my life began ;
> So is it now I am a man."

THE BRIDGE.

Did you ever walk beside a pretty stream with ferns and flowers upon its bank? Did you ever wish to cross the stream and find it too deep to wade and the stones too far apart for you to jump from one to the other? Did your papa or some strong man throw a board across and then lead you to the beautiful things on the other side?

Perhaps that is what the man in the picture is going to do with the boards he has on his shoulder. Find all the bridges you can in the picture. There is one just strong enough for an ant to cross; there is another for men, and one which a squirrel might use. You can make a bridge with your hands like the one in the upper part of the picture, but do not forget to use your thumbs for the support of the bridge.

The lily leaf has roots underneath, and the branch which the squirrel runs over is held by the trunk of the tree. Can you think of any other bridges that join things which would be separated but for them? Did you not get a letter from papa when he was away from home? Was not that a little bridge that brought his thoughts to you?

When you have been rude or unkind to any one did you not feel far away and unhappy? and were you not glad when kind words and loving smiles made a bridge by which you could return to happiness?

If you watch for the opportunity you can be a little bridge-builder every day, for you have in your heart that which must support every bridge.

You surely know what made the man carry the boards for the children; what made your papa write the letter? what made your mamma speak gently when you were cross?

Was it not love?

And does not love unite all parts of the earth as the bridge unites the opposite banks of the stream?

Was it not love in men's hearts that made them see in the rainbow a bridge which joined earth to Heaven?

HOW MANY BRIDGES DO YOU FIND IN THE PICTURE?

STAR MYTHS

IF you look at the sky any clear night this
month you may see a path of light nearly overhead, stretch-
ing from the northern to the southern horizon. This is called
the Milky Way, and in the old, old times children were told that it
was milk spilled by a baby god. It sometimes happens that there is
a starless night, and as these children of the ancient times believed
nothing was really lost, they had a story about the stars all leaving
the sky and alighting upon the tail-feathers of peacocks.

I wish all who read these stories would look at the stars this very
evening with the poetic feeling of the children of long ago.

Turn back to the April rain myths and you will see the six doves
which I told you would come back to us in the star myths. The
rainy sisters were said to have seven dear little sisters, who, because
they were so kind and good, were set in the sky as stars, which
sometimes looked like white doves. But we can see only six of

these stars, because one of them was so sorry for the sufferings of men that she turned her face away — and some believed she even went away from the sky forever.

There are a great many stories of men who were changed into stars and given a home in the sky, and one pretty one tells how a man went to bathe in a sacred river, and as soon as his body touched the river it was changed into a swan and taken up to Heaven, to be placed with other beautiful creatures among the stars. There are beautiful stories about all the brilliant stars which you can pick out in the Milky Way. If no one can tell them to you, you can make some for yourself, for you have all that is needed for making a good story if you feel the love which shines through the sun, moon and stars, and keeps our hearts full of joy, even in the darkest night.

The poet Tennyson wrote a verse which you will like to learn :—

" Many a night I saw the Pleiades rising through the mellow shade
Glitter like a swarm of fireflies tangled in a silver braid."

Another poet tells a story of a Star which rebuked a glow-worm for daring to show its little taper in the grass when the great lights were shining in the sky. While the Star was talking, a great storm arose, the hills shook, the rivers ran backward and a new sky, more beautiful than the old, suddenly appeared. And every star that spangled the new sky had been, but a moment before, a brave little glow-worm of the earth.

THE LITTLE GIRL AND THE STARS.

THE story in this picture is of a little girl who is looking at the stars with her mother and seeing two large and bright ones exclaims:

" See the father and mother stars ! "

Then the mother asks her to look at the little stars that are also shining so brightly, telling her that their light is perhaps less than that of the large stars, but that every light is needed up there, and helps us to see down here.

People have loved the stars so much that they have not only thought with the little girl that the stars loved each other as we do, but that the stars of the sky might have little brothers and sisters among the flowers of the earth. See the starry flowers in the picture, and when you go to walk and cannot see the stars overhead, look for them in the grass at your feet. There is a flower called Star of the Earth, and one cannot look at the asters this month without thinking of the blue sky and the silvery stars.

Even the ocean has its star-fish, and in winter the snow flakes form in star shapes, as if Nature herself loved this form.

What makes the stars shine ? Do you remember the rainbow bridge ?

The little ray of light comes all the way from the farthest star to tell us the same story of a love that lives among the stars as well as among the clouds. As the bridge found its rest in our hearts, so the star finds a light in our thoughts, and we are happy as the mother and child in the picture, who if they were to turn and look in each other's eyes, would see a light there which almost reveals what we can never quite see with our eyes — the love that shines when the sun, moon and stars are no longer with us.

There is more poetry about the stars than even your papa would like to learn. But a few lines of one of the very oldest poets you should know :

" Where wast thou when I laid the foundations of the earth ? When the morning stars sang together and all the sons of God shouted for joy ?

Canst thou bind the sweet influence of Pleiades, or loose the bands of Orion ? "

SEE THE FATHER AND MOTHER STARS.

HARVEST MYTHS

For out of the old fields as men saithe
  Cometh al this new corne fro yere to yere
And out of old bookes, in good faithe
  Cometh all this new science that men lere.
                    CHAUCER.

From the old books we will learn some of the harvest myths which people have believed. Most beautiful is that of Ceres who cared for all the grain, not for her own use, but for the sake of the earth people.

Children and poets of the Old World watched the coming and going of the seasons, and told each other pretty stories about the fruits and grains of autumn. When summer with its flowers gave place to the season which brings the ripened grapes and grain, these happy story-tellers said that a beautiful maiden who played with the flowers had gone away to some other country, taking with her the delicate spring violets and nodding anemones.

The corn and golden wheat growing in their

places were the gift of the graceful maiden's mother, the stately Ceres who had come to look in all the fields for her lost child. Many children forgot that these thoughts were only poetic fancies woven into lovely stories, and grew into believing them quite true, and after a time their pictures and statues and the very flowers themselves were thought sacred.

Some said the flower maiden had fallen asleep in another world, and so could not hear her mother call, and they brought poppy wreaths to hang upon the lovely carved images of the lost child. Of Ceres, her mother, they said: Bright-haired Aurora, when she came forth in the morning, and Hesperus when he led out the stars in the evening, found her still searching for her daughter.

One pretty story says Ceres once sat down upon a stone to rest and weep, but a little girl seeing her look so sad, very softly whispered: " Mother ! " and with that magic word Ceres arose and followed the child to her house, where she found a little boy lying very ill.

You will know almost without being told, that Ceres cured the sick child. When he was older Ceres came again, took him in her golden chariot and taught him things which he afterward taught men about the care of grass and grain.

It is most wonderful and beautiful that these myth-makers held one precious truth in all their wandering fancies. You will find it in their stories of the sun, moon and stars, whether told by Greek or Hindu, and we sometimes find it even now in the heart of a little child who never heard one of these stories :

Love never sat down to cry over its own troubles, or went seeking its own joy forgetting the needs of others. So Ceres, the goddess of the harvest, gave the golden corn and waving wheat to men as she passed across the earth in search of Summer, her darling flower-child.

Some tribes of Indians still believe that corn, beans and squashes have lives which remain in the forms of beautiful maidens who attend the yearly growth of these things.

If you can see a corn-field to-day, your mamma can find a story to tell you about the blessing of the corn-fields which Longfellow has so beautifully told in his poem of Hiawatha.

TICK TACK.

In this picture we see a clock and a baby. The baby's mother is teaching it to swing its arm to and fro like a clock pendulum. The clock tells the baby a great many things with its tick tack. In the morning it says: "Time to get up, time to get up, time to get up;" then it says, "time for your bath, time for your bath, time for your bath;" at noon it says, "time for dinner, time for dinner, time for dinner." When the day is fair it says: "Time for a walk, time for a walk, time for a walk." See the baby's crib: when the birds go to their rest the clock still talks; hear it; "time for the baby to go to bed, time for the baby to go to bed, time for the baby to go to bed."

The baby loves to watch the clock pendulum and swing its arms in time with it. There is a pretty song which you can learn and picture with your hands and arms.

"See the neat little clock, in the corner it stands
And points out the hours with its two pretty hands;
The one shows the minute and the other the hour
As often we see in the high church tower.

The pendulum swings inside the long case
And sends its two hands round its neat little face,
It never should go too slow nor too quick,
But swing to and fro with a tick, tick, tick.

So must I, like the clock, my face happy and bright,
My hands quick in motion must always do right;
My tongue must be guarded to speak what is true!
Wherever I go and whatever I do."

Fröbel, who gave us a number of tick-tack songs and games, wanted even the little children to obey the rule of the clock. We are happy if we do things the minute we are told to do them; and if we are in our places in kindergarten just at the right hour, that hour is pleasanter for us and for others. We spoil a song if we sing too slow or too fast. The very sun, moon and stars keep up the harmony of the skies by taking their places at the right hour.

BABY LOVES TO WATCH THE CLOCK.

FIRE MYTHS

HAVE you seen a maple-tree with leaves as red as fire? Have you looked at the glowing fingers of the sumach this month? Perhaps you have had a fire in the grate, and have watched the glow of the coals or the gleam of little red tongues of flame that go whirling up the chimney.

When men first saw fire, and before they had learned to kindle or keep it, what do you suppose they thought about it?

And can you think what fire they must have seen first?

It was the quick, lurid flash of the lightning. You have perhaps seen it dart down as from the heavens and touch a forest tree, setting it ablaze in an instant.

To these Old World children it was easily explained by some poet, who, if in the world now, would like his thought better than anything we could teach him about electricity. He said : "It is a bird with flaming crest and glowing wings ; it flew from the heavenly ash-tree and alighted upon one of our trees, and the glory of its presence has burned the earth tree to ashes." These Old World children did not like the thought of a beautiful earth tree becoming nothing but ashes, so what story do you suppose they devised for their own comfort?

Out of the ashes they said another bird arose, and all unseen by them, flew back to its heavenly home. From this pretty story there grew many others about the strange bird called a Phœnix. One fire bird was not enough, however, to satisfy these story-making and story-loving people.

Soon, any bird that flew swiftly, or had upon its wings or breast the color of fire, was said to be a lightning bird, and the eagle, king of birds, the woodpecker with his blazing crest and the robin with its red breast, all became sacred as bringers of fire. They soon learned that the sun also held fire, and when they at last learned how to rub two sticks of wood together until fire burst from one of them, it is no wonder they loved the man who was thought to have done it first. These Old World people would not be half so dear to us now had not their young world hearts been overflowing with love and deepest reverence for everything they saw in sky or tree. They were grateful for the warmth of the fire and all the ways it served their needs, but they could not take it and use it as if they had made it. It was no common gift, and from worshiping it and those who brought it, grew many beautiful religious customs. The sacred fire was never permitted to go out upon Hebrew altars.

A pretty legend tells of an infant prophet being thrown into the fire by a wicked ruler, whose evil purpose was defeated, for the bed of flame was instantly changed to one of roses upon which the baby slept unhurt before the very eyes of the man who learned that no harm could really befall the innocent. Every one of these beautiful things, sunshine and light of stars ; rainbow and singing breeze ; flower and shower finds its kindred spirit in our own joyous hearts that give back love for love to Him who rules them all.

THE PIGEON HOUSE.

WHAT do you see in this picture? I see four mammas and more babies than you can count.

Two that walk are coming down the road to tell their mamma what they have seen, and two that fly are telling where they have been and what they have seen.

The children coming from the field saw a man ploughing, and he showed them a ground bird's nest in the grass, which was so pretty he would not disturb it, though the little birds flew away weeks ago. They also saw many little creatures with wings which were not birds, and they are talking with each other about bees and butterflies, and the questions they will ask their mamma about the difference between bats and birds, and birds and moths, for they think everything that flies ought to be called a bird.

What do you suppose is in the basket?

They have been to the field, you remember. And you remember the man was ploughing this field. What do you think grew there this summer?

Wheat. And when the workmen cut and drew the wheat away, they dropped many and many a beautiful straw with its head of good wheat upon it, and these dear children have filled their basket with that golden grain so they will have the pleasure of feeding it to the pigeons.

The mother sitting near the pigeon house is teaching her little girl to play Fröbel's game of the Pigeon House.

You can fold your hands like these in the picture and then open one of them letting your fingers flutter about like pigeons.

The pigeons must be very happy this month, the world is so beautiful. Think what they see in their flight. Golden fruit, purple grapes, glowing leaves of red and gold, streams and bridges, corn-fields and rain-clouds. Perhaps pigeons' eyes can see the lovely woman you read about last month, who is still looking among the poppies for her little girl.

FOUR MAMMAS AND THEIR BABIES.

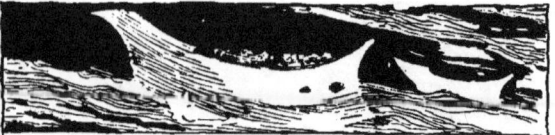

Cloud Myths

A NY child who will look at the clouds from day to day will be able to see pictures in them, quite as beautiful as those which the people saw when the world was young.

Men and women who lived in the country saw hills and meadows among the clouds, where sheep and cattle roamed.

When men and women lived in cities they fancied they saw cities among the clouds; they pictured radiant processions, cloud-capped towers, and soon they began to believe in a palace whose walls and chambers were gleaming in sun or moonlight.

No sooner did one see a palace than another thought it had golden doors and silver steps. Then, as the clouds floated aside, there seemed to be beautiful youths guarding the palace, with flaming torches in their hands.

Where one poetic child could see a youth with a torch, another could see a maiden with a golden distaff, and the threads she was spinning were woven into filmy clouds ; and as the clouds spread and seemed to sail across the sky, of course some one cried :

" A ship ! a ship ! "

What beautiful stories may be woven about a cloud ship! It might belong to the owner of the palace ; it might be Freya's bark ; it might be the divine Argo which could talk with the people and do the will of the gods without pilot or helmsman, rudder or rigging.

Freya's magic bark, they said, could be folded like a veil and carried in the hand, or it could become a powerful vessel with iron prow which no enemy could injure.

Sometimes the clouds grew black, and what seemed a glowing torch became like a raven ; and what had looked like a snowy sail seemed changed to a dragon's wing.

Watch the clouds for yourselves and you too will see pictures.

Perhaps you will see the Shining One, the Moon Maid, the Whispering Æolus, the Rainy Sisters or Freya's Tresses, for they are one and all but light and sound, shower and flower, dressed in the filmy garment of child-like thoughts about them ; and you may think these thoughts over again as you look into cloud-land, letting your imagination sail away with the Argos, flame in the torch, climb the silver stairs of the palace, or draw bright threads from the golden distaff.

THE FAMILY FESTIVAL.

THIS is the month of the family gathering.

The children visit grandpapa and grandmamma or uncles, and hear delightful stories of the childhood of papa, mamma, aunts and uncles. Grandmamma tells what she did when she was a little girl, and grandpapa tells the children how their papa behaved when he put on his first trousers.

The baby is filled with joy, because on this holiday mamma's first doll is taken from its little box in the drawer and the children are allowed to play with it, while stories are told of its dress which was made of a piece of grandmamma's wedding gown, and its slippers of grandpapa's gloves. This doll has laid tucked away in one of mamma's wedding slippers.

The children feel that the holiday would not be quite perfect without these stories of the children who used to play very much as they play now.

One of the children puts on grandmamma's glasses and another leans on grandpapa's cane, while auntie shows them a kindergarten finger-game :

"This is the grandpapa!
This is the grandmamma!
This is the father dear!
This is the mother dear!
This is the little child!
See all the family here?"

Or, touching thumb and fingers, in the same order, she sings :

"This is the mother good and dear;
This is the father with hearty cheer;
This is the brother stout and tall;
This is the sister that plays with her doll;
And this is the little one, pet of all!"

Of course everyone kisses the little finger which represents the baby, "pet of all."

THE FINGER FAMILY.

WINTER MYTHS

THE world was once believed to be a great ash tree: Beneath one of its roots lay a whole country peopled by giants, even the animals being of such gigantic size that a mosquito would be larger than one of our ostriches and a squirrel would be about the size of a very large elephant. Of course the tree had to be large and strong enough to hold such birds and squirrels, and the children were never little even when babies. Such was the belief of Norsemen. In this country of the giants lived the Father of Winter. His breath was so icy that everything froze before him as he walked; he wore a great cloak made of eagle's feathers, and if he but moved an arm cold winds rushed out and shook the great ash-tree in

every limb. As the cold increased in the winter of the north country, the people told each other wilder and wilder stories, and one long, dark night some merry boy or girl made up a story of a wolf in the giants' country that was so large he had swallowed the sun! Another said somebody would surely catch the wolf and take the sun away from him.

"Who could run fast enough to catch that wolf?"

"I," said Vidas, "I have magic boots."

"Where did you get magic boots?"

"They were made of all the bits of leather pared and cut from the heels and toes of all the shoes ever made," answered Vidas, and away he strode after the giant Fenris wolf. And he caught him, too, and made him open his mouth and give up the sun, and all the children shouted for joy when they saw Vidas hang the sun up in the sky again.

Other children told stories about the snow, saying a most beautiful woman with eyes like sapphires and footsteps soft and silent came in the night and wrapped the earth in a white mantle as a mother wraps her baby in its blanket of wool. There are children to-day who shout joyfully, "Frau Hulda has been here!" when they look out in the morning and find the earth covered with snow since they went up to bed. Last winter a little boy called to me in tones of delight: "See! see! the twinkle stars are falling!" He had caught some star-shaped snow crystals on his mitten.

The story of the Wolf and the Sun is one of the oldest stories known and is a hundred times prettier than a hundred others that have grown out of it. In telling you these many old, old stories of sun, moon and stars, I have taken the greatest care to give you the best ever told; and as you read and re-read them you will see that whether they grew up among Greeks or Hindus, Norse or Arabs, every one was stamped with a most beautiful, heaven-made feeling which finds an answering thought in the heart of every child. They are part of the world's old story, out of which all good stories grow, the story of love which makes gods and giants, fairies and children, men and women forget themselves in doing for others.

THE WINDOW.

WHEN you first wake in the morning, after kissing papa and mamma which way do you look? Nearly always toward the window, I am sure. Sometimes in winter the window shows you many beautiful pictures on it, as if it could not wait for you to come and look through it to see what is outside.

The frost makes many a fine drawing of mountains and castles, trees, flowers and ferns upon the glass.

In the illustration you see how you can make windows with your hands, and you will have great pleasure in peeping through the sash and telling stories of what you see. Sometimes our eyes are called the windows of our souls, and I am sure when you look in mamma's eyes you will see a light more beautiful than that of the sun from the window of your room. And now I am going to tell you something very wonderful about what may be seen in these eye-windows.

If a little boy with frowning brow and unhappy mouth looks deep into mamma's loving eyes what do you think he will see? Just a frowning, unhappy little boy, no matter how much mamma may wish him to see a happy one. It can be no other way.

Smile and look into the eye-window and you see a smiling face.

It is very much that way with every kind of window. The sun may shine into the clearest window that ever lighted a pretty room, but if you look through that window with your feelings all clouded and cross you cannot see the sunlight as the beautiful thing it is to the child who is in a pleasant temper.

So we really make our windows what we will. We may have them daintily traced with fairy-like pictures of beautiful scenery, like our house windows in a frosty winter morning, or we may see in them the glowing colors of the most lovely church window, or they may be so clear and unspotted that there seems nothing between our souls and the ever-near Soul of all Love. If you keep your soul like that, you will know the meaning of the windows and all you see through them, from stars in the sky to snowflakes on the sill.

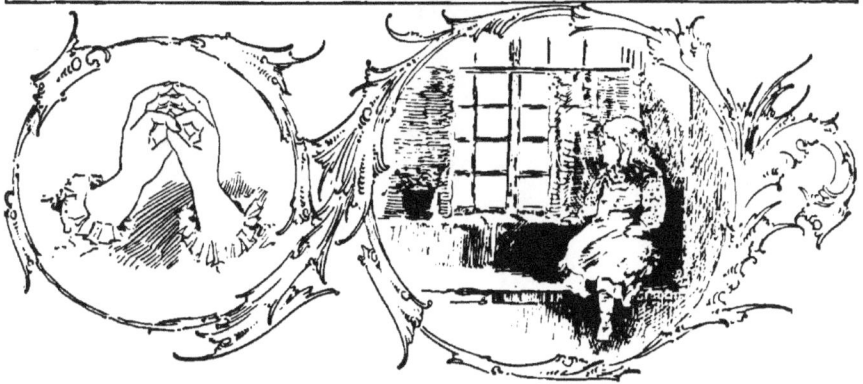

THE WINDOW.